The L.I.F.E series presents…

FAITHFUL STEPS

Experience the transforming power of following God

A 30-DAY DEVOTIONAL

Selena Bolton

Copyright ©2025 Selena Bolton

All rights reserved. No part of this book may be reproduced or used in any manner without the prior written permission of the copyright owner

Published by: Salt & Moon Books, USA

Paperback ISBN: 979-8-9933728-1-5

Cover Illustration Copyright © 2025 Selena Bolton

TABLE OF CONTENTS

INTRODUCTION	1
DAY 1 – FROM THE GARDEN TO THE WILDERNESS	3
DAY 2 – CHOSEN FOR ISOLATION	5
DAY 3 – F.E.A.R.	7
DAY 4 – CASE DISMISSED	9
DAY 5 – PERFECT GIFTS	11
DAY 6 – THE BICYCLE	13
DAY 7 – IF YOU BUILD IT	15
DAY 8 – THE BLUEPRINT	17
DAY 9 – A BIRD IN THE HAND	19
DAY 10 – A RAM IN THE BUSH	21
DAY 11 – ARE WE THERE YET?	23
DAY 12 – THE LIFE PRESERVER	25
DAY 13 – IN THE MEANTIME	27
DAY 14 – RUSHING THROUGH THE WILDERNESS	29
DAY 15 – MATH CLASS	31

DAY 16 – GOOD POSTURE	33
DAY 17 – WHISPERS IN THE WILDERNESS	35
DAY 18 – THE VOICE	37
DAY 19 – FOLLOW INSTRUCTIONS	39
DAY 20 – TAPPED OUT	41
DAY 21 - CALLED OUT	43
DAY 22 – SINGIN' IN THE RAIN	45
DAY 23 – REST STOP	47
DAY 24 – GET DRESSED	49
DAY 25 – SURVIVAL OF THE FITTEST	51
DAY 26 – A CHANGE OF HEART	53
DAY 27 – THE EASY WAY?	55
DAY 28 – RENEWED MIND	57
DAY 29 – RENEWED VISION	59
DAY 30 – RENEWED COMMITMENT	61

INTRODUCTION

The Wonders of the Wilderness

Many of us believe that we end up in wilderness places because we've been disobedient, and the wilderness is a form of punishment. This devotional declares: **it's not the wilderness that is the issue, it's the wandering**. In Matthew 4, we see that the Holy Spirit *led* Jesus into the wilderness. In Jeremiah, the exiles were *instructed* to build and bear children in the wilderness (Jeremiah 29:5-7).

In this same way, you and I will be called to follow God into wilderness seasons. The wilderness, though it may seem lonely, builds new levels of faith, trust, obedience, and intimacy with the Lord. Contrary to popular belief, we need wilderness moments; the key is to walk through in obedience—**you were never meant to wander**! (Proverbs 3:6)

Are You Wandering?

God is silent, but your kids aren't. God seems far away, but your bills are on your back. God called you, and then it seems He abandoned you. You've quoted every scripture you know and sung every song on your Spotify playlist. Your situation doesn't look much different from how it was last year. You feel lost; the life you've envisioned, the life God promised, seems out of reach. You're not alone (Joshua 1:9), you could be experiencing a wilderness season. Let's take *Faithful Steps* through this place together!

Let's pray:

Father God, thank You for Your presence and grace. Throughout this study, give us a greater understanding of Your Word, an appreciation for Your people, and an increase in the fruits of Your Spirit. As we work through these pages, may Your character be magnified and Your name be glorified. Be with us through the wilderness and lead us into all Truth. In Jesus' name, we pray. Amen.

DAY 1 – FROM THE GARDEN TO THE WILDERNESS

"Teaching them to observe all things whatsoever I have commanded you: and, lo, I am with you always, even unto the end of the world. Amen." (Matthew 28:20)

The Garden of Eden: A place of beauty, tranquility, and eco-prosperity. The place God chose to put "the man He had formed" (Genesis 2:8). A place of comfort and security. Adam's only job was to take care of the land and give the animals names (Genesis 2:15-18). There was only one rule: do not eat from one certain tree. God made Eve for Adam, and they tended the garden daily.

Ease and comfort didn't last long, though. They eventually broke the only rule they had and were exiled to a world of struggle. The Garden of Eden was a divine place of communion with God, where one could learn who He is and build a relationship with Him. It's not so easy to get along with God nowadays, is it? We have work, family, school, health, bills — the list of concerns and responsibilities is endless.

So, where can we go to cultivate a deeper relationship with God?

The wilderness. The wilderness is not a physical location, but rather a spiritual one. In the wilderness, we commune with God and are molded and shaped 'in His image'. However, God doesn't commune with our human nature. To commune with the spirit, He put in us (James 4:5), He has to relieve us of things: our dependence on the world, our dependence on ourselves, our desire for self-indulgence.

When you find yourself feeling alone and things in your life seem fruitless and empty, chances are, you've been called into a 'wilderness season'. Let God lead you through it; trust Him to provide for you and keep your eyes on Him. Your promised land is on the other side!

Reflection: *How can you acknowledge a need for God? How can you follow His lead instead of relying on yourself?*

DAY 2 – CHOSEN FOR ISOLATION

"And Mary said, Behold the handmaid of the Lord; be it unto me according to thy word. And the angel departed from her." (Luke 1:38)

Breath of Heaven, a narrative song by Amy Grant, tells the story of a frightened Mary--confused but trusting God to be with her while she obeys the call to give birth to the Messiah. The words of the song bring us right into the loneliness that oftentimes accompanies obedience. Mary asks God to lighten the darkness she feels in her moments of uncertainty. She's willing, but in need of comfort.

Mary's son, God's only begotten Son, would echo this same sentiment in the Garden of Gethsemane before His crucifixion (Matthew 26:39). In obedience, Jesus was desperately alone in the garden of Gethsemane (Philippians 2:8). For her obedience, Mary was "put away" (Matthew 1:19); how isolated they must have felt. Nevertheless, they followed through with what was being asked of them.

As Christians, we should model this same sacrificial trust and obedience. Mary, still a virgin, gave birth to the hope of the entire world! Jesus, the embodiment of that hope, died a cruel and humiliating death to atone for every sin of every person who has and will ever live!

Know this: when God asks anything of us, it is always tied to something bigger than us. Think about that when you feel the pull to obey the Lord. Jesus asks us to "take up [our] cross" and follow Him, to do as He did (Matthew 16:24).

This is how wilderness moments shape us. When you find yourself "put away" or in the "place of pressing", ask God to be near you, to pour his comforting holiness over you.

Let's pray now: *Father God, just as You were with Mary, and just as You were with Jesus, be with us. We want to obey, help us obey. We want to serve, strengthen our hands. Thank you, Lord, for your Holy Spirit that keeps us and empowers us to do Your will. May our lives bring you glory. In Jesus' name we pray, Amen.*

DAY 3 – F.E.A.R.

"Yea though I walk through the valley of the shadow of death, I will fear no evil, for you are with me; your rod and your staff, they comfort me." (Psalm 23:4)

You're home alone in bed and hear noise. Now you hear footsteps. The wind outside is howling like a hungry coyote. Suddenly, a loud crashing noise comes from the front of the house. It's dark, but you see someone crouching in the corner of your room. You grab your phone, and that's when you see it. The figure huddled in the corner…is actually just a pile of clothes. The noise you heard? Whiskers, your cat, knocked a cup off the kitchen counter. You laugh at your runaway imagination and go back to sleep.

When facing a time of spiritual fortification, the first thing you may feel is fear. While this is a very normal human emotion, the Bible tells us that it is not God's intention for us to live in that fear (2 Timothy 1:7). Someone once said, F.E.A.R. stands for: **F**alse **E**vidence **A**ppearing **R**eal. False evidence can be what we see with our eyes or the beliefs we hold in our hearts. So, how can we know if what we are 'seeing' is real?

It is through our knowledge, environment, and past experience that we inform our vision of reality. When we are home alone, we lock our doors because we know that home invasions happen. As believers, we know that Jesus died for us so that we can live for Him; this informs our decisions and guides our behavior. We should read the Bible to understand God's character (knowledge), surround ourselves with worship and prayer (environment), and reflect with gratitude on all that the Lord has done (past experience). Fear doesn't stand a chance when we understand that it is the counterfeit cousin of FAITH!

Reflection: *What do you know to be true about who God is? How can that knowledge sustain you in uncertain times?*

DAY 4 – CASE DISMISSED

"As for God, his way is perfect; the word of the Lord proves true. He is a shield for all who take refuge in him" (Psalm 18:30)

Several years ago, I met Korey Wise while wandering the streets of Harlem, New York. Korey, along with four other young boys, had been convicted of a brutal attack on a woman in Central Park in 1990. The corrupt investigation, faulty trial, and erroneous verdict have been the subject of the media for years. After years in prison, Wise and the others were exonerated due to DNA evidence that backed a confession from the real attacker. They are free!

We have also seen false accusations all throughout the Bible. Satan accused God of trying to deceive Adam and Eve (Genesis 3:4-5), the apostle Paul was accused of going against the law (Acts 21:28), the servant blamed his master in the parable of the talents (Matthew 25:24-25), Potiphar's wife accused Joseph of attempting to assault her (Genesis 39:6-14) and the Pharisees constantly accused Jesus of all manner of wrongdoing.

You and I can be like those false accusers of Biblical times. When things don't go our way, we accuse God of not loving us, we say He is cruel and unfair. As we learned yesterday, this happens because we do not know God intimately. We have not searched the scriptures to sufficiently root ourselves in the truth. We don't routinely exercise our faith to see evidence of His hand moving on our behalf. We seldom relinquish control long enough to obey Him, and we often don't humble ourselves through consistent worship and praise.

The burden of proof of goodness is not on God; He does not change (James 1:17). The case we build against God's character will always be dismissed once the truth is revealed through His Word. Get to know the Lord today and become His witness, not His prosecutor.

Let's Pray: *Father, forgive us when we accuse You of being anything but good. We know that your ways are not like our ways. We can trust Your faithfulness to us and Your love for us. Thank you for the grace You show us as we learn to serve You.*

DAY 5 – PERFECT GIFTS

"Every good and perfect gift is from above, coming down from the Father of the heavenly lights, who does not change like shifting shadows." (James 1:17)

We sing about the goodness of God every week in church services around the globe. Whether you're a pew-warmer, active member, or "Streaming Saint" (thanks to the internet), you've sung about how good God is. You sang passionately from your heart because you were experiencing His love and faithfulness. Then, something life-altering happens, and the period at the end of "God is good" turns into a question mark, "God is good?" we suddenly ask.

Despite the good we know and have experienced, there will always be opposition to fully believing in God's divinely perfect character. Satan, the father of lies (John 8:44), is on a mission to distort the truth and deceive us. If he can get us to believe lies about God, he can persuade us to doubt God's true nature, power, and intentions toward us. Satan planted seeds of doubt about God's character from the very beginning: in the Garden of Eden. As soon as the Father's character came into question, disobedience and separation followed (Genesis 3:1-7).

The truth is, as James 1:17 tells us, everything 'good and perfect gift' comes from God. His gift-giving is a relationship-building tool designed to fulfill His Word and demonstrate His faithfulness. When we're going through a wilderness time, we need all the reminders we can get of God's goodness to us. He is the same yesterday, today, and forever. Today, tell God what traits you love most about Him. Tell Him how you experience Him. Go to the Word to learn more.

Reflection: *What good gifts can you look back on and see God's love for you? How did those gifts change your relationship with God?*

DAY 6 – THE BICYCLE

"Be imitators of God, as beloved children" (Ephesians 5:1)

On a recent FaceTime call with one of my brothers, he recounted a story from our childhood. One that illustrated who he would become — a powerful man of God. The story he told was of the day he won a bicycle in a raffle at our neighborhood bakery.

The Bakery Thrift Shop: all the kids flocked there, coins clutched in their little fists to buy pastries of every kind. My brother was no different; he saw the shiny new bicycle on display amongst the fresh-baked treats and declared, "I'm gonna win that bike!" No one held their breath, but he held onto what he knew. The rules stipulated that to enter the raffle, you must put your name on the back of your receipt and place it in the raffle box. So, my brother did just that, every chance he could, until the raffle ended.

Arriving home from school one day, our dad said the bakery called…MY BROTHER WON THE BIKE! Hearing my brother retell the story, I can't imagine any possession meaning more to him at that moment or even now. He told me on that FaceTime call, "My receipts were my faith. I couldn't have won the bike without putting those receipts in the box." (Whoa.)

Looking back, even at an early age, my brother understood the principle of James 2:26, which tells us that "faith without works is dead." Had my brother not believed he would really get the bike, his actions would have most certainly looked different. His belief dictated his actions; his actions indicated his faith. The bicycle was God's FAITHFULNESS to my brother.

Reflection: *Are you believing God for something that seems impossible? Check your 'receipts'. How are you showing the Lord you believe He can do what you've asked and believe? Are your actions reflecting your faith?*

But without faith, it is impossible to please him: for he that cometh to God must believe that he is, and that he is a rewarder of them that diligently seek him. (Hebrews 11:6)

DAY 7 – IF YOU BUILD IT

"So, then faith comes by hearing, and hearing by the word of God." (Romans 10:17)

In the movie *Field of Dreams,* Kevin Costner portrays a man plagued by a voice telling him, "If you build it, he will come." *Spoiler alert*: he, in fact, did build "it"—a baseball diamond in the middle of his cornfield. Once built, the miracle of faith, obedience, and love culminated in the greatest game he'd ever witnessed.

The wilderness is a place of purpose, where we intentionally seek to be alone with God. To hear instructions from Him. To discipline our minds and purify our motives. To prepare us for service and blessing. The wilderness is also a place of grace; we go there to prevent ourselves from taking matters into our own hands. Alone with Him, our senses are sharpened, our discernment heightened, and our intimacy deepened. If we are obedient in the wilderness, we will see His glory in all areas of our lives.

What is God calling you to do? Does it sound absurd? Impossible? That's the thing God is asking you to believe. Your purpose in life reaches far beyond what you're wishing for; God's glory is revealed in your purpose. I'll bet Costner's character in *Field of Dreams* had no idea how the voice he heard, and the invitation to "build it" he received would test his faith, change his life, and the lives of others.

Reflection: *How can you take a step of faith forward and trust the Lord through the wilderness? What will you build for God's Kingdom?*

Now faith is the substance of things hoped for, the evidence of things unseen.

(Hebrews 11:1)

DAY 8 – THE BLUEPRINT

"Walk in obedience to all that the Lord your God has commanded you, so that you may live and prosper and prolong your days in the land that you will possess". (Deuteronomy 5:33)

The teacher passes out the tests, and everyone begins working. "Turn in your test as soon as you're finished," she says. Thirty seconds later, more than half the class walks to the front of the room to submit their work. The others look up from their tests, wondering how their classmates could be finished so quickly. Those still seated had failed to read the instructions: *To pass the exam, ONLY print your name. Failure to read the instructions will result in a failing grade.*

Now, let's go back in time. Imagine being instructed to build a big boat because soon, the entire earth would flood. Noah was a righteous man in a sea (pun totally intended) of disobedient people. God gave Noah the blueprint that would save his life and the lives of his family (Genesis 6:14-16). By faith, he would restore all of humanity; I'd like to think of him as the "architect of obedience.

But imagine if Noah had brushed off God's instructions. What if he said, "Hey! I have an idea, God. How about we don't do that? It hasn't rained in years, and I'll be the laughingstock of the neighborhood". Or, what if he decided that gopher wood was too expensive, so he bought materials that couldn't withstand the flood waters? Disaster!

Today, the gravity of disobedience is hardly feared by believers because we've become too comfortable with the "God of grace". God indeed gives much grace, but that grace is given to us so that we can relentlessly pursue righteousness. His instructions have an end goal: for us to live a life that is pleasing to Him.

Reflection: Following instructions can be difficult. Think honestly: What's a barrier to your obedience to God? Dare to follow instructions and watch God's blessings flow!

"Whoever gives heed to instruction prospers, and blessed is he who trusts in the LORD" (Proverbs 16:20)

DAY 9 – A BIRD IN THE HAND

But seek ye first the Kingdom of God, and his righteousness; and all these things shall be added unto you. (Matthew 6:33)

The TV game show "Let's Make a Deal" was popularized in the 1960s, entertaining families across the U.S. Host Monty Hall would call on contestants to accept what they already had in their hands or give it up for an unknown prize. This put the saying, "a bird in the hand is worth two in the bush," to the test.

Our faith in God's provision is often put to the very same test: give up what we can see and touch, in exchange for some unknown outcome. On the surface, we know that faith is the "substance of things hoped for" and the "evidence of things unseen" (Hebrews 11:1), so why do we hold on so tightly to what's in our hands when the Lord prompts us to surrender it?

Well, I can tell you what it was for me. I had exercised the muscle of self-reliance for far too long and had become prideful in my ability to do things for myself. My lack of trust in humans had bled over into my relationship with God. I worked when I could have been resting in (Philippians 4:19). Instead, I spent forty proverbial years of wandering through the wilderness of my best efforts.

You've had moments like this, too, where you've contemplated: stay at your current job or get a new one, move to another city/state/country, or stay put; divorce or remain married; continue serving in ministry or step down. The list is endless, and the choices can be life-altering. The fear of uncertainty tempts us to accept what's in our hands, right now, rather than trusting what seems just out of focus--and reach.

Thankfully, we don't have to "make a deal" with the Lord. We can take him at His Word (Isaiah 55:11). He **will** supply all our needs.

Reflection: *So, will you set the bird free, lift your empty hands, and take hold of, by faith, what the Lord has for you?*

"Consider how the wildflowers grow. They do not labor or spin. Yet I tell you, not even Solomon in all his splendor was dressed like one of these." (Luke 12:27)

DAY 10 – A RAM IN THE BUSH

"Abraham answered, "God Himself will provide the lamb for the burnt offering, my son." (Genesis 22:8)

Yesterday, we talked about "a bird in the hand" symbolizing what we could provide for ourselves. We have all experienced the false sense of security that self-reliance can bring. Self-reliance works well in a world that values "pulling yourself up by your own bootstraps", but that mentality is in direct conflict with a life lived for the Lord. (Proverbs 3:5-6) Now, let's go back to that bush, but instead of two birds being in it, there is a ram.

God had instructed Abraham to take his beloved son, Isaac, up on Mount Moriah and sacrifice him (Genesis 22:2). In that moment, Abraham knew two things: the instruction came from the God he served, and Abraham knew that same God was going to provide for him. After what I'm sure was an agonizing journey, Abraham and Isaac finally reached the mountaintop. Abraham prepared his child to be killed, raised his knife, and…the test abruptly ends with a sacrificial ram instead of his child! (Genesis 22:9-11)

This is God's provision! God gives in ways that can only be attributed to Him.

I wonder what would have happened on Mount Moriah if Abraham had doubted God and packed a "backup sacrifice" just in case. Thankfully, he didn't, and his obedience now stands as a testimony of what God can and **will** do when we put our complete faith in Him.

Reflection: *Have you ever had an 'eleventh-hour ram' show up in the bushes for you? How can you use that instance to fortify your faith for future tests and trials? Are you ever tempted to have a backup plan "just in case"?*

DAY 11 – ARE WE THERE YET?

"I am sure of this, that he who started a good work in you will carry it on to completion until the day of Christ Jesus." (Philippians 1:6)

One thing many parents can agree on is that embarking on a road trip with children can be an ambitious undertaking. You're traveling about twelve hours away, and only 30 minutes into your travels, you hear something from the backseat. "Are we there yet?!" Yep, it's going to be a looong trip.

Our lives with Christ can feel a lot like a long road trip, leaving us constantly asking, "Are we there yet?" "There," in eternal terms, of course, is heaven. I don't think any of us are asking if we are in heaven yet, though.

The "there" most of us are referring to is some unmet need that we have. It could be a financial need (*"Lord, aren't you gonna bless me with some money yet?"*). It could be an interpersonal need *("Lord, it's me again, I'm tired of being alone, where is my wife/husband?")*. It could even be a spiritual need *("Lord, yeah, hi. Me again. Is it possible to let me have a little joy?")*

Are we **there** yet?!

"There", at its core, is the place we feel that God is favoring us, we are in right standing with Him, and we are finally free from struggle. This is unrealistic because the Bible tells us that we **will** have trouble in this world (John 16:33).

Maybe the more productive question is, "Am *I* yet?" Am I reflecting Your image as I live my life? Am I being obedient to your Word? Am I humbly serving Your people? Am I free from selfish ambition and worldly desires? The question of "Are we there yet?" implies that we are passively on our way somewhere with little to no control. "Am I yet?" implies that we are actively participating in making our way to eternity with the Lord.

"Looking unto Jesus the author and finisher of our faith; who for the joy that was set before him endured the cross, despising the shame, and is set down at the right hand of the throne of God." (Hebrews 12:2)

DAY 12 – THE LIFE PRESERVER

"Hope deferred makes the heart sick, but a longing fulfilled is a tree of life." (Proverbs 13:12)

When the Lord called me to focus on writing, I was jobless and on the verge of homelessness. He reminded me that the fulfillment of His purpose for my life was ensconced in my obedience to His instructions. I worried every day about my basic needs, even though I knew by heart the scripture that says not to worry about those things (Matthew 6:31-32).

Perhaps you're working two jobs while attending school full-time. Maybe you're on the first day of sobriety. Maybe you're trying to improve your failing health. What's motivating you to continue? It's hope, isn't it? Why else would you hold on? You hope your situation will improve. You hope to be rewarded for your dedication.

Hope is such a powerful force that Proverbs 13:12 tells us delaying it will make "the heart sick". Think of being promised something, but you're not sure when you're going to get it. The days and weeks turn into years, and still nothing. Paul prayed about this for the Romans, "*May the God of hope fill you with all joy and peace as you trust in him, so that you may overflow with hope by the power of the Holy Spirit*" (Romans 15:13).

Look at that! God fills us with joy and peace as we learn to put our trust (and hope) in Him. He wants to be the focus of our hope. Hope **in Him** decreases our worries, and trust **in Him** increases our joy. Refocus your hope because God's Word is true and His promises will ALWAYS be fulfilled (Isaiah 55:11).

Let's pray: *Father God, we put our hope in You and trust You to provide for us, even in uncertain times. Help us to turn to you as the source of all hope and give us the strength to endure. Thank you for being the author and finisher of our faith.*

"But they that wait upon the LORD shall renew their strength; they shall mount up with wings as eagles; they shall run, and not be weary; and they shall walk, and not faint." (Isaiah 40:31)

DAY 13 – IN THE MEANTIME

"Build houses and settle down; plant gardens and eat what they produce." (Jeremiah 29:5)

"We wanted to let you know that management is moving forward with your promotion: 50% salary increase, new corner office, two weeks of additional paid vacation, and a flexible working schedule. Congratulations!" "Finally!" you silently retort. Your boss continues, "However, we haven't yet determined when this will take effect. **In the meantime**, keep up the great work."

What? How long will you have to wait?!...

The Bible illustrates a similar 'in the meantime' scenario in the book of Jeremiah. In Jeremiah 29, the exiles were anticipating being brought out of captivity (suffering and uncertainty) and into the land promised to them and their descendants—a prosperous place they had been told was 'flowing with milk and honey'. Instead, Jeremiah reads them a letter in which the Lord instructs them to create families and build while they're in the wilderness. (Jeremiah 29:5-6) Talk about a momentum killer!

Today, many of us (especially in this era of the 'self-help/prosperity gospel') love to quote Jeremiah 29:11. But what about the verses before that? Jeremiah 29:4-13 gives us a clear picture of the true intent of that overly-quoted eleventh verse. Jeremiah 29's message is the epitome of "in the meantime". God asked them to continue living productive lives, even though all they wanted to do was reach the Promised Land.

The words of the Lord in Jeremiah 29:11 aren't at all about a magic genie promising the holder of the lamp three wishes. They are a call to action: trust the Lord in the meantime—an exercise of faith, patience, and obedience to His Word.

Reflection: *How can you be productive in a 'meantime space' and still maintain your faith in the future promised to you?*

"For I know the plans I have for you," declares the Lord, "plans to prosper you and not to harm you, plans to give you hope and a future" **(Jeremiah 29:11)**

DAY 14 – RUSHING THROUGH THE WILDERNESS

"For everything there is a season, and a time for every matter under heaven" (Ecclesiastes 3:1)

Holding onto the promise of returning to New York City to live as a writer had become too much to carry, so I started bargaining. I would ask the Lord if I could "just go visit" to "stay inspired." He would be silent; I would keep asking. "No," He finally said. *I can just pretend I didn't hear that. God understands that I'm not perfect, right? What's the harm?* Well, let's take a look at a Biblical example.

When the Lord promised Sarai and Abram that they would have children, Abram "believed God and it was counted to him as righteousness" (Genesis 15:6). Sarai, however, required a bit more convincing; she grew impatient. If God wouldn't give her a son, Sarai would get a son on her own. That's when she hatched a plan: she would ask her servant, Hagar, to be with Abram and conceive a child for her. The result was a whole lot of strife between the three and merciful intervention from the Lord (Genesis 16:4-6; Genesis 17:1-7)

Sarai's refusal to wait led to a broken relationship with Hagar, a son born to Abram from Hagar who was not his intended heir, and family drama that would rival that of the Hatfields and McCoys. Through it all, God had surely intervened, but what if His grace hadn't been so abundant? The consequences would have been the end of an entire lineage, one that included Jesus Christ Himself.

This is another divine purpose of the wilderness; it shapes us into who we need to be to carry the promise and purpose God intended for us. Remember, God's timing is always intentional, and His leading is always beneficial (Romans 8:28). It is to our benefit to walk *with* the Lord through tough times and not ahead of Him. If we are wandering through the wilderness, we miss the blessing of deliverance. Conversely, rushing through the wilderness, we miss the blessing of the growth and strength needed to sustain us.

Reflection: *What has being in a hurry cost you in the past? Are you waiting right now? How can you exercise more faith, trust, and patience?*

"The plans of the diligent lead surely to abundance, but everyone who is hasty comes only to poverty" (Proverbs 21:5)

DAY 15 – MATH CLASS

The Lord will rescue his servants; no one who takes refuge in him will be condemned. (Psalm 34:22)

Subtraction: *Footprints in the Sand* (*authorship attributed to several different people) is a poem about someone recalling their life's journey and always seeing two sets of footprints—they knew that the Lord was with them. But during very trying times, they only saw one set of footprints. They questioned why the Lord would abandon them in their times of need. The Lord answered, "The times when you have seen only one set of footprints, my child, are when I carried you."

Addition: Shadrach, Meshach, and Abednego also have a story of God's powerful presence, which began with their refusal to bow to an idol commissioned by King Nebuchadnezzar (Daniel 3:1-30). When confronted, the young men stood their ground and were immediately thrown into a blazing furnace. However, they were not burning at all. In fact, a fourth man could be seen standing by the fire with them. The flames of the furnace were extinguished, and Shadrach, Meshach, and Abednego emerged from the furnace without even the scent of smoke on them!

The story of Shadrach, Meshach, and Abednego highlights God's faithfulness; His faithfulness to deliver those who are faithful to Him. *Footprints in the Sand* highlights God's grace; His grace to carry us through challenging times. As an act of faith, carve out daily time for worship. Worship keeps our focus squarely on the Lord, not on our problems. Worship transfers the obligation to solve the problem from us to the Lord (1 Peter 5:7). When it's not adding up, lift Him up!

Reflection: *What else can you do to endure fiery trials? How can you exercise faith and trust during challenging times?*

"Rejoice always, pray continually, give thanks in all circumstances; for this is God's will for you in Christ Jesus." (1Thessalonians 5:16-18)

DAY 16 – GOOD POSTURE

"Trust in the Lord with all your heart and lean not unto your own understanding" (Proverbs 3:5)

In every class, in every interaction with my adult ESL students, I had become combative and intense. Anxiety about my future had me desperately searching for control anywhere I could find it; the students had unwittingly become my targets.

Being a tutor became less about service and more about paying my bills. Unconsciously, I began to physically lean forward in my chair when they spoke. I was ready to pounce and whip them into shape should they not conform to my unspoken demands and needs (Those poor students).

Walking with the Lord can have some of those same anxiety-inducing moments, can't it? He speaks, and what we see in front of us runs completely contrary to the Word we received by faith. He says, "Wait," our situation says, "Hurry up!" He says, "Trust me," our situation says, "Figure out, now!" What do we do in those moments of anxiety and even fear? Take the proper posture.

Proverbs 3:5 calls us to that posture, one of prayer, worship, and a readiness to obey. Following God requires a level of humility that doesn't come naturally to us because we are hardwired to "figure it out". But what a gift we have! We can lay at God's feet His authority and His power. He will deliver us.

Reflection: *What is your posture saying to the Lord? How can you posture yourself to truly listen and obey what the Lord is saying? How can a grateful heart improve your posture?*

"And we know that all things work together for the good of those who love him, who have been called according to his purpose" (Romans 8:28)

DAY 17 – WHISPERS IN THE WILDERNESS

"Christ learned obedience through the things he suffered" (Hebrews 5:8)

Have you ever seen a TV show where a character faces a problem and must make a difficult choice? All of a sudden, an angel appears on one shoulder, and a pitchfork-toting devil shows up on the other. The angel, with a sweet operatic voice, encourages the character to do the right thing. Meanwhile, the devil, with villainously arched eyebrows and a mischievous grin, presents his case for why the character should do the obviously wrong thing.

In our lives, this scenario often plays out. Give that one coworker a piece of your mind. Smoke that cigarette just this once. Cheat on your spouse. Cheat on your taxes. Life is full of choices. How can we be sure we hear God's voice clearly? How can we resist the urge to give in to temptation? The answer is in the wilderness.

In the wilderness, Jesus, hungry after forty days without food, withstood Satan's taunting and tempting. Satan slinked up to the Messiah, "If you are the Son of God, tell these stones to become bread" (Matthew 4:3). Jesus used the Word of God to defeat the enemy with each subsequent attack. Satan fled, and angels came and ministered to Jesus (Matthew 4:11). This is a powerful demonstration of the authority we can have over temptation.

Temptations come in many forms. When the whispers of temptation come, speak the Word. Even if it's only one verse you know, say it! Do you want to experience victory in your life? Know the Word, speak the Word, and live by the Word (Matthew 4:4).

Let's Pray: *Lord, we are grateful for your Word. Your word defends us, saves us, and sustains us. Help us to live, not by bread alone, but by every word that comes from Your mouth. Thank you for empowering us to resist the devil and his temptations.*

"Get thee behind me, Satan! For it is written, "Worship the Lord your God and serve Him only..." (Matthew 4:10)

DAY 18 – THE VOICE

"The righteous cry out, and the Lord hears them and rescues them from all their trouble" (Psalm 34:17)

"Hi, yes, may I please speak to someone about this overcharge on my bill? Thank you so much."

We sometimes refer to this as our "customer service voice." You know the voice: you're really brooding with irritation on the inside, but if you show that, it's game over. So, you put on your best, calmest voice and attempt to get what you need.

In our prayer life, we can have this same customer service voice. You know the one, "Dear Heavenly Father, you are so good. Thank you for your blessings. Please continue to bless me…" Our prayers are perfectly pitched and punctuated. This is especially evident in church services; those who lead prayers tend to have a propensity for sounding pious, holy, and articulate.

However, what Jesus taught on prayer was clear: "And when you pray, do not be like the hypocrites, for they love to pray standing in the synagogues and on the street corners to be seen by others. Truly I tell you, they have received their reward in full (Matthew 6:5). The focus of our prayers should be to reach heaven, not each other.

Instead, Jesus said we should go to our room, shut the door, and pray. Our private prayers to God will be heard (and rewarded) according to His will (Matthew 6:6). The Bible says that people will size us up and measure us by our outward appearance, but God looks at the heart (1 Samuel 16:7). You're safe with God. He created you. He knows you. He loves you. Go to God with your heart; ask for help, being vulnerable and honest. Prayers of sincerity are the ones that move the hand of God.

Let's Pray: *Our Father, who art in Heaven, hallowed be thy name. Thy Kingdom come, thy will be done on earth as it is in Heaven. Give us, this day, our daily bread and forgive us our debts as we forgive our debtors. And lead us not into temptation, but deliver us from evil. (Matthew 6:9-13)*

"I call on the Lord in my distress, and he answers me." (Psalm 120:1)

DAY 19 – FOLLOW INSTRUCTIONS

"Man shall not live by bread alone, but by every word that proceeds out of the mouth of God." (Matthew 4:4)

My dad recently showed me a package of MREs he had saved from his days in the military. MREs, or Meal, Ready-to-Eat, were pre-packaged meals rationed to military personnel during times of combat or when they were out in the field. Some call them daily rations because they were not meant to be feasts, but just enough to sustain you for each day.

The Israelites also had daily rations. While traveling through the wilderness, the Israelites started complaining of hunger. So, the Lord made food rain down from heaven (Exodus 16:13-15). Manna. Divine provision. Moses instructed the Israelites to only gather what they and their families could eat for the day; they were not to keep any of it until morning. Did they listen? Nope, not everyone. Some of them hoarded food away, but by morning, it had spoiled and was full of maggots. (Yikes!)

The spoiled food points to what happens when we fail to follow instructions. The lesson was to trust God daily, to follow Him and look to Him to provide (Philippians 4:19). Some of the Israelites thought they knew better than what they were told to do, so they did their own thing. If they had just listened, they would have gotten so much more than food!

When we follow God's instructions, our spirits grow stronger (Isaiah 1:19). We develop the faith, trust, and love necessary to live lives full of peace and victory. There are certainly going to be times in our lives when we only have enough for the day: enough food, enough money, enough strength, enough patience. In those moments, look to heaven with full faith and watch the manna rain down!

Reflection: *How can you show God that you trust Him for your daily bread? Do you need to surrender self-reliance?*

"And my God will meet all your needs according to the riches of his glory in Christ Jesus." (Philippians 4:19)

DAY 20 – TAPPED OUT

"...To obey is better than sacrifice, and to heed is better than the fat of rams." (1 Samuel 15:22)

Yesterday, we saw what happens when we are careless with God's provision. Today, we'll see what happens when we are careless with God's power. It's not good, I can tell you that.

As was their habit, the Israelites had been complaining. This time, it was about the lack of water on their journey through the Desert of Zin (Numbers 20:1-2). So, God instructed Moses to speak to a rock, and it would bring forth water to quench the thirst of the group. Instead, out of frustration with the complaining masses, Moses hit the rock twice to produce water. What was the consequence of Moses' refusal to follow instructions? He and Aaron would be kept out of the Promised Land forever (Numbers 20:12). You may be thinking, "Wow, that seems harsh!"

This isn't just about the method of getting the water itself, though. Miracles bring glory to God and deepen the faith of those who witness them. By Moses tapping the rock in anger, he brought attention to himself. His disobedience showed his lack of faith in the Lord and denied God the opportunity to show Himself to the people.

We can fall into the same trap Moses did when we're frustrated, when we're exhausted from our kids or boss complaining, when we're tired of waiting for things to get better, when we have had enough of things going wrong. Our emotions often get the best of us, and we stray from what the Lord wants for us.

Next time you're surrounded by frustration and uncertainty, try praise. Praising God turns our focus from our circumstances to God. The Bible says in God's presence, there is fullness of joy (Psalm 16:11); praise brings us into that presence. This is not to say that we should deny our problems exist; that's impossible. But filling our hearts and homes with praise sets the stage for God's miracles to take place in our lives.

"Better is one day in your courts than thousands elsewhere" (Psalm 84:10)

DAY 21 - CALLED OUT

"Oh, you of little faith! Why did you doubt?" (Matthew 14:31)

Used as an icebreaker, team-building exercise, or couples therapy demonstration, the "trust fall" is a valuable tool. In the trust fall exercise, one person stands with their back turned to another person (or group of people). Then, the person with their back turned falls back into the waiting arms of the other person (or people). That's it, that's the exercise. Easy, right?

The Bible demonstrates a version of the trust fall in the book of Matthew. While sailing with the other disciples, Peter tells Jesus, "If it's really you, call me out of the boat to come to you." "Come," Jesus says. When Peter looks down and realizes he's defying logic, he begins to sink. Peter had looked at his surroundings and not at his Lord. After saving Peter, Jesus asks him, "Why did you doubt?" not because Jesus needed an answer. The question was an invitation for Peter to examine his own heart.

It's noteworthy that Peter was a disciple of Christ and presumably knew Jesus in ways the masses did not. Even so, it seems that Peter couldn't reconcile what he *knew* about Jesus with what he was *seeing* in the waters surrounding them. This is why faith is the "evidence of things unseen" (Hebrews 11:1). Peter's knowledge of who Jesus is seemed insufficient for Peter to trust Jesus, proving that knowledge alone is not enough. Knowledge builds trust, experience builds faith, and obedience builds intimacy.

In times of uncertainty and isolation, we often find ourselves like Peter; we crave reassurances of who the Lord is in our lives. When we ask Him to show up and prove Himself, what is revealed first is what's in our own hearts. So, before calling out for the Lord to show Himself, be sure you're ready to step out of where you are.

"When I am afraid, I put my trust in You" (Psalm 56:3)

DAY 22 – SINGIN' IN THE RAIN

"Rejoice always, pray without ceasing, give thanks in all circumstances; for this is the will of God in Christ Jesus for you." (1 Thessalonians 5:16-18)

Musical theater makes every situation seem glamorous, exciting, and beautiful. Even when something tragic happens, we are escorted through it with pageantry and spectacle. Don't you wish all of life's problems could be solved in under three hours with an intermission for snacks?

I have often wished my life were like a perfectly choreographed production. In real life, I feared trials because I didn't think I was strong enough to withstand them. I feared happiness because I didn't know if sadness or pain was lurking around the corner waiting to engulf me. A life worth living seemed like a far-off dream until I went to the scriptures in search of truth.

The truth is that Jesus addresses this existential dread throughout the scriptures. In Luke 12, Jesus instructs the listener not to worry about "what you will eat or drink". He says to "seek ye first" the Kingdom of God, and all those things will be added. God is with us always (Matthew 28:20); He will never leave or forsake us (Deuteronomy 31:8).

We can live life without being resigned to fear or anxiety (2 Timothy 1:7) because we live in the Truth. The truth is that trouble will come, but it doesn't last (Psalm 30:5). We can bury our past under the cross of Christ's sacrifice and entrust our future to God the Father. What good would Christ's victory over death be if we lived as if we were defeated? So, cry when you need to cry, laugh when you have the chance, and love God, yourself, and your neighbor with all your heart.

Life is not a musical, but it can be one filled with songs of hope, faith, love, and gratitude.

Let's Pray: *Father, thank you for being our joy! Help us to have a greater understanding of what it means to "rejoice always." When we don't have the words, hear our hearts. When we can't find a smile, be our joy. Thank you for taking such good care of us now, and always.*

DAY 23 – REST STOP

"So, he said to me, 'This is the word of the LORD to Zerubbabel: 'Not by might nor by power, but by my Spirit,' says the LORD Almighty." (Zechariah 4:6)

What discourages believers and unbelievers alike is the impossibility of perfection that we think God requires. Believers get frustrated at the recurrence of sin in their lives; never seeming to be "holy" enough to be considered a "true Christian". Unbelievers are repelled by what seems to them a never-ending list of dos and don'ts. But the truth gives us hope and invites us into a place of peace.

In his song "Strength of the Lord," Larnelle Harris sings about God's strength being found in trusting, resting, and praying. What a powerful revelation to have and hold on to! The words of this refrain of vulnerability reveal the true nature of a relationship with God. Following God often requires us to rely on concepts that are completely counterintuitive to our human nature (but isn't that the point? Difficult, still, I know.)

The strength to endure all the ups and downs of life is found in the Holy Spirit's power, in the mercy of God, and in the sacrifice of Jesus. Are you living in that truth today? Or are you still trying to be good enough?

Reflection: *When you are tempted to start 'doing' your Christianity, ask God to reveal your heart to you. Ask Him to show you where that striving is coming from, surrender that part to God for deliverance and healing.*

"Being confident of this, that he who began a good work in you will carry it on to completion until the day of Christ Jesus." (Philippians 1:6)

DAY 24 – GET DRESSED

"For we wrestle not against flesh and blood, but against principalities, against powers, against the rulers of the darkness of this world, against spiritual wickedness in high places." (Ephesians 6:12)

The po' boy sandwich is quintessential New Orleans cuisine. French bread sliced in half and filled with your choice of seafood, roast beef, hot sausage, or…you get it. Your protein choice is then topped with lettuce, tomato, pickles, and mayonnaise. To get the full experience of a traditional po'boy, you should ask for it 'dressed'.

As Christians, we are also called to be 'dressed'. Not in pickles and mayo, of course. We're to be dressed in the whole armor of God (Ephesians 6:13-17). Like the elements of the po' boy, each piece of armor serves a unique purpose.

We should be doing a daily 'fit check.' Do you have your belt of truth? Your breastplate of righteousness? How about those gospel shoes? Don't forget your shield of faith, helmet of salvation, and sword of the Spirit (which is the Word of God). What is the function of each piece?

- The belt of truth combats lies and deception

- The breastplate of righteousness guards your heart from bitterness
- The shoes of the gospel of peace usher in the hope of salvation to those you meet
- Your shield of faith is vital! It puts out Satan's fire
- The helmet of salvation guards the mind and keeps your thought life pure
- The sword of the Spirit, the Word of God, is the greatest tool in your arsenal

How can we be sure we're properly outfitted every day? Prayer! The word of God says to pray in the Spirit on all occasions with all kinds of prayers (petitions, praises, intercessions, etc.). Pray for God to help you 'get dressed' every day and watch Him help you overcome every obstacle!

Pray This: *Lord, thank you for giving me a way to protect myself from spiritual attacks. Help me to get dressed every day and to stand firm in my faith. Guide me onto the path of truth and give me grace to continue serving you daily.*

DAY 25 – SURVIVAL OF THE FITTEST

"He that loves his life shall lose it and he that hates his life in this world shall keep it unto life eternal." (John 12:25)

Life can resemble the *Hunger Games*, where one lives to merely survive another day. Survival mode implies that something, or someone, is in danger of dying. When we say we are in survival mode, it's usually our psychological or financial well-being we're referring to. However, there is also a spiritual survival mode that we can find ourselves in.

Spiritual survival mode is a struggle between the flesh and the spirit. Paul knew this struggle well: "I do not understand what I do. For what I want to do I do not do, but what I hate I do." (Romans 7:15). Living this way starts with the fallacy that we are in control over every facet of our lives. Believing that we have the ability to have, be, and do whatever we want with all the desired outcomes we want. We think if we struggle, it's because we somehow failed; if we succeed, then fight tooth and nail to remain successful (because we think we control that, too).

There's no room for God to operate in this framework; He becomes a footnote to our story. He becomes the bargaining chip we use to get and keep ourselves away from struggling. This is the mindset that has to die in the wilderness. God's divine wisdom in leading the Israelites through the wilderness to get to the Promised Land is inspiring. He knows that time in the wilderness is imperative to getting rid of self-reliance and cultivating God's reliance (Hebrews 5:8). Self-reliance dies in the wilderness—what lives is trust in the Lord. Idol worship dies in the wilderness—what lives is God's glory.

Let's Pray: *Father God, thank you for being someone we can rely on. We put our trust in You to provide for us in every way, so that we are free to serve You. We ask You now to deliver us from putting our trust in surviving, for loving our earthly lives more than an eternity with You. Purify our hearts and let hope in You be the joy that carries us through each day. In Jesus' name we pray. Amen*

"For he that soweth to his flesh shall of the flesh reap corruption; but he that soweth to the Spirit shall of the Spirit reap life everlasting." (Galatians 6:8)

DAY 26 – A CHANGE OF HEART

"But you, O Lord, are a God of compassion and mercy, slow to get angry and filled with unfailing love and faithfulness." (Psalm 86:15)

While sitting around chatting with the community's social pariahs (tax collectors) and other sinners, Jesus told a series of stories, known as parables. In one parable, two sons were living with their father. The younger asked his father for his inheritance; the young son then left to spend it as he pleased (Matthew 15:11-12).

Cocky and newly wealthy, he spent lavishly and recklessly. He ended up broke and at the end of his rope. To survive, he got a job feeding some pigs, though he himself was starving. Realizing that he had reached his rock bottom, he decided to go home (Matthew 15:17-20). But something was different…

Gone was the cocky attitude, and in its place, contrition. The prodigal son was willing to go home and be one of his father's servants. The young man hung his head and began his journey home, no doubt trying to imagine the life of servitude that lay ahead. But instead of being met with judgment, the father welcomed his young son home with open arms, fresh clothes, and a ton of delicious food (Matthew 15:20-24)!

God has the same heart; He loves to see us run to Him, ready to submit to His plan for our lives. He longs to have us back home in the safety of His Spirit and perfect will. Repentance is the key to reclaiming our Kingdom inheritance. Our hearts are ready to serve God and not self. Hearts fully committed to moving forward in righteousness, never to return to our old ways. *Is your heart truly repentant?*

Surrender today: *Dear Lord, give me a contrite and repentant heart. Show me the things I need to surrender and give me the strength to overcome temptation. Thank You for the grace that helps me to do what honors You.*

DAY 27 – THE EASY WAY?

"Now the Lord is the Spirit, and where the Spirit of the Lord is, there is freedom" (2 Corinthians 3:17)

I am hesitant to write this entry because it has the potential to come across like a bright and shiny advertisement *("Accept Jesus and you too can live happily ever after!")*. The truth is, living for Jesus can be challenging, not because of rules, not even because of the myriad temptations we face daily. No, it is difficult because we are learning daily how to live contrary to our desires.

Desire is a powerful force. So much so, Paul questioned himself and his seeming inability to exercise self-control (Romans 7:15-20). To be clear, desire is neither good nor bad; it is the *object* of our desire that determines its merit and outcomes (Colossians 3:2).

Before accepting Christ, we lived by a different code of conduct; that doesn't necessarily mean we were living reckless or immoral lives. However, it does mean we were living lives outside of what God intended for us. For Christians, anything that takes our attention away from living a God-honoring, Christ-led life is a temptation.

This is the purpose and the power of wilderness moments: Transformation. We are in the wilderness learning how to surrender to God's will and leadership. We're relieved of all that is harmful or unnecessary—old mindsets, attitudes, beliefs, and behaviors.

To embrace God's will, we must first accept His Son. Upon accepting His Son, we must commit to surrendering our old lives, just as we would an expired passport. We're new, and as with anything new, living by a different standard is a process. The longer we live in our new freedom, the less we will desire our old life (2 Corinthians 5:17).

"Come unto me, all ye that labor and are heavy laden; and I will give you rest. Take my yoke upon you and learn of me, for I am meek and lowly in heart. And ye shall find rest unto your soul. For my yoke is easy and my burden is light." (Matthew 11:28-29)

DAY 28 – RENEWED MIND

"Do not conform to the pattern of this world, but be transformed by the renewing of your mind. Then you will be able to test and approve what God's will is—his good, pleasing and perfect will." (Romans 12:2)

The Israelites were freed from a life of bondage marked by the cruelest, most brutal conditions (Leviticus 26:13). In order to get to the prosperous place promised to them (Ha! Say that three times fast), they would need to follow Moses and Aaron through the wilderness. In the wilderness, fertile ground and sufficient water were in short supply, which made the journey tedious and long. Many scholars believe that the journey only required a couple of weeks. Instead, it took the Israelites 40 years! Why?

Disobedience and distrust. They didn't trust the process, their leaders, or their God, and nothing was ever good enough for them. The Israelites were constantly looking to the past instead of focusing on what lay ahead; they longed for their old lives, when the new life seemed too distant. Today, how can we go from our old life through our wilderness to our new lives?

We renew our minds by acquiring new information. By studying the scriptures to understand God's character and what He wants you to do, and how He wants you to live. By listening to that often still, small voice of the Holy Spirit. By living in service to God, not the other way around. This is life in Christ.

If we want to live in the newness of life with Christ, we must commit to a new way of thinking. We must trust that God is who He says He is (Hebrews 11:6); surrender to His leading (Psalm 32:8) and have faith in the fact that He has a plan (Jeremiah 29:11).

Reflection: *Living for the Lord requires a new way of thinking. Can you commit to daily scripture reading and prayer? Ask God for His help; remember, you're not alone.*

DAY 29 – RENEWED VISION

"Where there is no vision, the people perish: but he that keepeth the law, happy is he." (Proverbs 29:18)

We talked yesterday about the importance of a renewed mind when serving the Lord, and we've learned that the power of faith lies in seeing what we believe. This brings us to the next step: renewed vision.

In order to follow God, we must be able to see Him. This sounds obvious, but how many of us think that our Christianity lies in seeing ourselves (*we are good, we are holy, we are righteous*)? This is where Proverbs 29:18 often gets misused.

Prosperity preachers and well-meaning folks want you to think that the verse is encouraging us to get a vision for ourselves. This is false. The vision we need is for the righteousness of God's law and commands (Jeremiah 7:23). How else are we to follow Him?

I'll admit, I was professing Christ long before I was actually following Him. My mind was not renewed, and I lived for many years believing that believing was good enough. For some, it may be, but I was stumbling around in the dark trying to figure out what God wanted from me until I had enough…

"Okay, God, listen. I'm only sure of three things: You are God. You have a son named Jesus who is our Savior. I know the Holy Spirit is real. The rest of this stuff, you're going to have to teach me. I'll listen." This prayer, said out of earnest frustration, sent me straight into a wilderness season. Once there, the Lord began to reveal Himself to me and show me who He wants to be in my life.

Get honest with God today, ask Him to renew your mind and give you eyes to see where He's leading you.

Let's Pray: *Father God, thank You for Your Word, which is filled with Your truth and encouragement for the journey of following You. Give us eyes to see and ears to hear. Purify our hearts so that we have a willingness to serve You. Thank you for Your faithfulness to us.*

DAY 30 – RENEWED COMMITMENT

"Commit thy way unto the Lord; trust also in him; and he shall bring it to pass." (Psalm 37:5)

All this talk about the wilderness would lead you to expect the end of this study to usher us into the Promised Land. After all, isn't that the whole point of the wilderness? Let's look, instead, at all we've experienced up to now.

We entered the wilderness in need of liberation, redirection, and purification. In the wilderness, we learned how to increase our faith in God, cultivate intimacy with God through trust-building, and identify and obey His instructions.

The spiritual cycle of walking in the wilderness and liberation will repeat itself throughout our entire lives. As long as we live in these bodies, there will always be a need for God to call us away to be alone with Him, periodically. There is no shame in that (Romans 8:1); it's part of the human condition to stumble.

How we approach those times will determine if we wander aimlessly or march triumphantly through. The measure of our faith is how quickly we get up and how committed we remain to walking tall and strong.

Let's renew our commitment to take faithful steps with the Lord today!

Let's Pray*: Father God, thank you for guiding us through this study on the wilderness seasons of our walk with you. Help us to put into practice all that we have learned. By your grace, help us to live a life that brings glory to Your name. Let every season, every trial and test, and every blessing be a testament of your power and sovereignty. We love you, Lord, and thank You for all You are and all You've done. In Jesus' name, Amen.*

www.ingramcontent.com/pod-product-compliance
Lightning Source LLC
Chambersburg PA
CBHW032057040426
42449CB00007B/1113